My Family

CELIA BERRIDGE

Kingfisher Books

Story by Angela Royston

Kingfisher Books, Grisewood & Dempsey Ltd,
Elsley House, 24–30 Great Titchfield Street,
London W1P 7AD

First published in 1988 by Kingfisher Books

Words copyright © Grisewood & Dempsey Ltd 1988
Illustrations copyright © Celia Berridge 1988

All rights reserved

BRITISH LIBRARY CATALOGUING IN PUBLICATION DATA
Berridge, Celia
   My family.—(Stepping stones 1, 2, 3).
   1. Families – For children
   I. Title   II. Royston, Angela   III. Series
   306.8′5
ISBN: 0 86272 391 4

Cover design by Pinpoint Design Company
Edited by Vanessa Clarke
Editorial assistant: Camilla Hallinan
Phototypeset by Southern Positives and
Negatives (SPAN), Lingfield, Surrey
Printed in Spain

That's me in the mirror. I have fair hair, and a blue bear on my pyjamas.

My brother has fair hair like me. He is older than me and bigger too. Look, he is building a rocket. It's almost as high as me.

We have lots of fun playing together. Sometimes we jump on the bed to wake Mum up. "You little monsters!" she groans.

I like doing things with Mum.
Sometimes we read together in bed.

I like dressing up in her clothes.
Look how big her shoes are on me.

Dad is up already. He is making our breakfast. Please can I have some milk in my cup?

I like watching television with Dad.
We sit together in his big armchair.

My brother and Mum and Dad are my family, and this is our dog. We say he is part of our family, but really he just lives with us.

There are more people in our family,
but they don't live with us.

Granny and Grandad live near us and we often visit them. They are my Dad's parents.

Their house is full of interesting things to look at. But we have to be careful not to knock anything over.

Tick tock, tick tock! Grandad opens the grandfather clock so I can see the pendulum and the weights inside.

I like helping Granny in the garden.
Granny is very good at growing things.
Mum says she has green fingers.

I have another Granny as well. She is my Mum's mother, and I call her Gran. Gran lives a long way away but I often talk to her on the telephone.

Sometimes I send Gran one of my pictures, and she sends me a postcard.

My cousins and my aunt and uncle are coming to see us today. Uncle is Mum's brother. He is giving her a big hug.

Two of my cousins are twins. They are the same age and they look the same.

I like my big cousin Kathcrine best because she plays with me.

I hold on tight when she carries me on her back. Look how tall I am now.

The twins only play with my brother.

What a lot of noise we make when we are all together!

Now Dad is taking a photograph of all the cousins together. "Say cheese!" he says, and we all smile.